THE REPUBLIC OF LIBERIA

FOUNDATIONAL WORDS OF OUR NATION

Presented by

AHTIA Solutions, Inc.

ISBN-10:1545098506
Published by

www.improved2life.com

For more information contact

AHTIA SOLUTIONS, Inc.
Phone: 678.235.4524
Email: info@athiasolutions.com
athiasolutions@gmail.com
Web: www.ahtiasolutions.com

ACKNOWLEDGMENTS

For an important effort such as this project, many people at several levels need to share the credit. It is hoped, however, that a symbolic list may serve as a deserving honor to all these contributors. On behalf of AHTIA Solutions, I thank, from the bottom of my heart, all unnamed and named contributors to this civic education project. Special thanks go to Mr. Alphonso Tarue for his insight, which gave birth to the project; the president of the Liberian Association of Metropolitan Atlanta, Mrs. Yahsyndi Martin-Kpeyei, for her logistical support; and Professor Dr. K-Moses Nagbe for his editorial suggestions. We are also indebted to graphic designer, Mr. Frank Z. Morris, for the graphic design of the front cover.

Founded in 2013, AHTIA Solutions is a 501 (c) 3 organization dedicated to providing information technology and creative problem-solving solutions to everyday issues facing most developing countries or emerging economies.

Sincerely yours,
Dennis Jah
Co-founder & CEO, AHTIA Solutions

MAP OF THE REPUBLIC OF LIBERIA

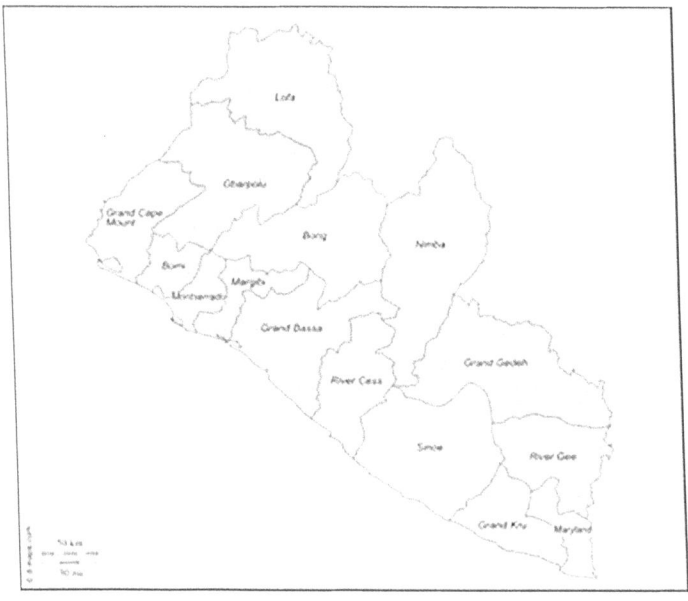

THE SEAL OF LIBERIA

The seal shows a sailing-vessel approaching the coast, a palm tree, a plow and a spade on the shore, a dove on the wing with an open scroll in its claws and the sun just emerging from the waters. Above the emblem is the national motto: THE LOVE OF LIBERTY BROUGHT US HERE. Beneath the emblem is the name of our country "REPUBLIC OF LIBERIA."

The ship represents the means by which the freed slaves traveled from the United states to Liberia. The palm tree symbolizes the products of the Republic. The spade and the plow symbolize the dignity of labor and hard work through which the nation will flourish. The dove on the wing with the open scroll in its claws shows that by the means of peace prevailing throughout the republic, knowledge shall be disseminated among all its inhabitants. The rising sun symbolizes the birth of a new nation.

FOREWORD

A MAJOR PART OF the pride which citizens of every nation show is their excitement to understand the basic makeup of the country, including the various power structures. This means getting the knowledge of who does what to keep the country safe and moving in the right direction, from one generation to another. The things to know and understand include a promise of respect to and defense of the nation, the nation's praise songs, its announcement to the world, declaring that it was free from physical control by any other nation or institution, and the body of principal laws that should guide how citizens behave to one another and how leaders of the country should behave to every other citizen who is not in leadership of the country. With regard to the praise songs in the book, a major one is the national anthem. The announcement to the world is called the Declaration of Independence. The body of principal laws is called the constitution.

THIS LITTLE BOOK THAT you are about to read contains the listed important documents of the Republic of Liberia— the serious promise to respect and defend the nation, two praise songs, the Declaration of Independence, and the Constitution. The information in the book has been arranged in such a way that you can carry the book in your pocket. Do you want to know words of the serious promise (i.e., the Pledge of Allegiance)? Do you want to know words of Liberia's National Anthem? Do you want to know what was said in the announcement declaring Liberia as a free nation on July 26, 1847? Certainly, the early people who established Liberia, later joined by those Africans met in Africa, were under the support and control of a major goodwill organization called the American Colonization Society. After sometime, these early people thought it was necessary to emphasize that they did not need the direct control and support of the organization. This refusal to be further controlled by ACS was the founding fathers' way of declaring independence. Do you want to know the principal laws of Liberia, which will help you know your basic rights and responsibilities? Then pay attention to every word in this little book. It will keep you informed about the various power structures. At the end of the book, you will be asked some questions, just to make sure you understand what you read. It's part of the fun. Whatever question you don't answer right, you can always go back to review the material.

KNOWING IMPORTANT THINGS ABOUT one's country is part of what is called the civic duty. It means you are showing that you are willing to understand that you are an important part of the community. No doubt, talking about a nation is like talking about a community, except that a nation is bigger than one's neighborhood, which may comprise of fewer houses and fewer people. All the same, a nation comprises of numerous houses and numerous people. You are likely to hear about some of these people on the radio, see them on TV, see them in the streets, see them in the market, see them in the mosque, at church or at any other worship center. You are likely to see some at school, soccer, or basketball games. How well you interact with all these people in all these places, will determine your willingness to develop and sustain peace in the country. As you may know, the more a nation is at peace, the more it can make significant progress from one generation to another.

WE SHOULD THANK AHTIA Solutions, a Liberian group, and the various supporters who have made this little book possible. May many others join them to make sure that we, Liberians and supporters of Liberia, understand these national documents so well that together we'll live in peace and work so much for the benefit of the Republic of Liberia.

It was my happy duty to say these few words about the little book. May we continue to love and treasure this one and only home God gave to us in West Africa.

K-Moses Nagbe, PhD
A RESEARCH LAWYER,
NOVELIST AND POET

TABLE OF CONTENT

Before you read this book, think about these questions and come back to answer them after reading

Why was Liberia established and has that original purpose being achieved?

What does it mean to be a Liberian?

Who is a Liberian?

As a citizen, what are my rights and responsibilities?

OUR OATH AND OUR SONGS

This section of the little book contains an oath and two well-loved songs of the country. Don't forget that an oath is a serious promise made either to do a specific thing or to avoid doing that specific thing. In the case of the oath, which is referred to as "The Pledge of Allegiance," all Liberians are making a serious promise that they will defend Liberia, no matter what it takes.

Then, there are two songs, which are the "Liberian National Anthem" and the "Lone Star Forever." Make sure to know the words and treasure them!

THE PLEDGE OF ALLEGIANCE

I pledge allegiance to the Flag of Liberia

And to the Republic for which it stands

One nation, indivisible with Liberty and justice for all

THE NATIONAL ANTHEM

[Lyrics written by President Daniel Bashiel Warner – 1815-1880, 3rd president of Liberia; and music by Olmstead Luca – 1826-1869. It became the official national anthem in 1847.]

All hail, Liberia, hail—
All hail!
All hail, Liberia, hail—
All hail!

This glorious land of liberty
Shall long be ours!
Tho' new her name
Green be her fame
And mighty be her pow'rs—

Tho' new her name
Green be her fame
And mighty be her pow'rs—
And mighty be her pow'rs
And mighty be her pow'rs:
In joy and gladness

With our hearts united

We shout the freedom of a race benighted—

Long live Liberia

Happy land!

A home of glorious liberty

By God's command—

A home of glorious liberty

By God's command!

All hail, Liberia, hail—

All hail!

All hail, Liberia, hail—

All hail!

In union strong success is sure

We cannot fail!

With God above our rights to prove

We will over all prevail—

With God above our rights to prove

We will over all prevail—

We will over all prevail

We will over all prevail:

With hearts and hands

Our country's cause defending

We meet the foe

With valor unpretending—

Long live Liberia

Happy land—

A home of glorious liberty

By God's command—

A home of glorious liberty

By God's command!

THE LONE STAR FOREVER

*[Written in 1901, at the age of 19, by Edwin J Barclay –
President 1930 – 1944; Born January 5, 1882 – died November
6, 1955.]*

When freedom raised her glowing form
On Montserrado's verdant height
She set within the doom of night,
'Midst lowering skies and thunderstorms
The Star of Liberty!

And seizing from the waking morn
Its burnished shield of golden flame
She lifted it in her proud name
And roused a nation long forlorn
To nobler destiny!

The lone star forever,
The lone star forever!
O long may it float
Over land and over sea—
Desert it, no never!
Uphold it, forever!
Oh shout for the lone-starred banner
All hail!

Then speeding in her course along
The broad Atlantic's golden strand
She woke reverb'rant through the land
A nation's loud triumphant song

The Song of Liberty!

And o'er Liberia's altar fires
She wide the lone-starred flag unfurled
Proclaimed to an expectant world
The birth of Africa's sons and sires
The birth of Liberty!

Refrain

The Lone Star forever,
The Lone Star forever!
O long may it float
Over land and over sea—
Desert it, no never!
Uphold it, forever!
Oh shout for the lone-starred banner
All hail!

Then forward, sons of freedom, March!
Defend this sacred heritage!
The nation's call from age to age
Where'er it sounds 'neath heaven's arch
Wherever foes assail
Be ever ready to obey
'Gainst treason and rebellion's front
'Gainst foul aggression in the brunt
Of battle lay the hero's way
All hail, Lone Star, all hail!

Refrain

The Lone Star forever,
The Lone Star forever!
O long may it float
Over land and over sea—
Desert it, no never!
Uphold it, forever!
Oh shout for the lone-starred banner
All hail!

THE SACRED DOCUMENTS
OF THE LAND

This section of the little book contains two very special documents. The first is the announcement made on July 26, 1847 about Liberia's independence. From that date forward, these repatriated Africans from the United States of America will not be living under the direct control of the American Colonization Society. They were now free!

The second document is the body of principal laws of the country. These laws, it should be remembered, are intended to guide all citizens. All citizens need to know how to behave to one another. They should know what to expect from their leaders; the leaders, too, should know what to expect from the citizens. Ignoring or defying these laws can become life or death matters for an entire country. Courts should make sure that no defiant leader or citizen gets away with defying these laws. Well-meaning groups of citizens should make sure that no one gets away with defying these laws. Having experienced a military coup and over a decade of civil war, mainly because these laws were either defied or ignored, Liberians apparently don't need any more preaching. All Liberians should never stand by unconcerned.

THE DECLARATION OF INDEPENDENCE

A DECLARATION OF Independence by the Representatives of the People of the Commonwealth of Liberia in Convention Assembled. July 16, 1847.

WE, THE REPRESENTATIVES of the people of the commonwealth of Liberia, in convention assembled, invested with the authority of forming a new government, relying upon the aid and protection of the Great Arbiter of human events, do hereby in the name and on behalf of the people of this commonwealth, publish and declare the said commonwealth a free, sovereign, and independent state, by the name and title of the Republic of Liberia.

WHILE ANNOUNCING TO the nations of the world the new position which the people of this Republic have felt themselves called upon to assume, courtesy to their opinion seems to demand a brief accompanying statement of the causes which induced them, first to expatriate themselves from the land of their nativity and to form settlements on this barbarous coast, and now to organize their government by the assumption of a sovereign and independent character. Therefore, we respectfully ask their attention to the following facts:

WE RECOGNIZE IN all men certain inalienable rights; among these are life, liberty, and the right to acquire, possess, enjoy, and defend property. By the practice and consent of men in all ages, some system or form of government is proved to be necessary to exercise, enjoy, and secure their rights, and every people have a right to institute a government, and to choose and adopt that system, or form of it, which in their opinion will most effectively accomplish these objects, and secure their happiness, which does not interfere with the just rights of others. The right, therefore, to institute government and powers necessary to conduct it is an inalienable right and cannot be resisted without the grossest injustice.

WE, THE PEOPLE of the Republic of Liberia, were originally inhabitants of the United States of North America.

IN SOME PARTS of that country we were debarred by law from all rights and privileges of man - in other parts, public sentiment, more powerful than law, frowned us down.

WE WERE EXCLUDED from all participation in the government.

WE WERE TAXED without our consent.

WE WERE COMPELLED to contribute to the resources of a country which gave us no protection.

WE WERE MADE a separate and distinct class, and against us every avenue of improvement was effectively closed. Strangers from other lands, of a color different from ours, were preferred before us.

WE UTTERED OUR complaints, but they were unattended to, or only met by alleging the peculiar institutions of the country.

ALL HOPE OF a favorable change in our country was thus wholly extinguished in our bosoms, and we looked with anxiety for some asylum from the deep degradation.

THE WESTERN COAST of Africa was the place selected by American benevolence and philanthropy for our future home. Removed beyond those influences which oppressed us in our native land, it was hoped we would be enabled to enjoy those rights and privileges and exercise and improve those faculties which the God of nature has given us in common with the rest of mankind.

UNDER THE AUSPICES of the American Colonization Society, we established ourselves here, on land, acquired by purchase from the lords of the soil.

IN AN ORIGINAL compact with this society, we, for important reasons, delegated to it certain political powers; while this institution stipulated that whenever the people should become capable of conducting the government, or whenever the people should desire it, this institution would resign the delegated power, peacefully withdraw its supervision, and leave the people to the government of themselves.

UNDER THE AUSPICES and guidance of this institution which has nobly and in perfect faith redeemed its pledge to the people, we have grown and prospered.

FROM TIME TO time our number has been increased by immigration from America, and by accession from native tribes; and from time to time, as circumstances required it, we have extended our borders by the acquisition of land by honorable purchase from the natives of the country.

AS OUR TERRITORY has extended and our population increased, our commerce has also increased. The flags of most civilized nations of the earth float in our harbors, and their merchants are opening an honorable and profitable trade. Until recently, these visits have been of a uniformly harmonious character; but as they have become more frequent and to more numerous points of our extended coast, questions have arisen which, it is supposed, can be adjusted only by agreement between sovereign powers.

FOR YEARS PAST, the American Colonization Society has virtually withdrawn from all direct and active part in the administration of the government, except in the appointment of the governor, who is also a colonist, for the apparent purpose of testing the ability of the people to conduct the affairs of government, and no complaint of crude legislation, nor of mismanagement, nor of mal-administration has yet been heard.

IN VIEW OF these facts, this institution, the American Colonization Society, with that good faith which has uniformly marked all its dealings with us did by a set of resolutions in January, in the year of our Lord one thousand eight hundred and forty-six, dissolve all political connections with the people of this Republic, returned the power with which it was delegated, and left the people to the government of themselves.

THE PEOPLE OF the Republic of Liberia, they, are of right, and in fact, a free, sovereign, and independent state, possessed of all the rights, powers, and functions of government.

IN ASSUMING THE momentous responsibilities of the position they have taken, the people of this republic feel justified by the necessities of the case, and with this conviction they throw themselves with confidence upon the candid consideration of the civilization of the world.

LIBERIA IS NOT the offspring of ambition, nor the tool of avaricious speculation.

NO DESIRE FOR territorial aggrandizement brought us to these shores; nor do we believe so sordid a motive entered into the high consideration of those who aided us in providing this asylum. Liberia is an asylum from the most grinding oppression.

IN COMING TO the shores of Africa, we indulged the pleasing hope that we would be permitted to exercise and improve those faculties which impart to man his dignity; to nourish in our hearts the flame of honorable ambition; to cherish and indulge these aspirations which a beneficent Creator had implanted in every human heart, and to evince to all who despise, ridicule, and oppress our race that we possess with them a common nature; are with them susceptible of equal refinement, and capable to equal advancement in all that adorns and dignifies man. We were animated by the hope that here we should be at liberty to train up our children in the way that they should go; to inspire them with the love of an honorable fame; to kindle within them the flame of a lofty philanthropy, and to form strongly within them the principles of humanity, virtue, and religion.

AMONGST THE STRONGEST motives to leave our native land - to abandon forever the scenes of our childhood and to sever the most endeared connections - was the desire for a retreat where, free from the agitation of fear and molestation, we could approach in worship the God of our fathers.

THUS FAR OUR highest hopes have been realized. Liberia is already the happy home of thousands who were once the doomed victims of oppressions; and, if left unmolested to go on with her natural and spontaneous growth, if her movements be left free from the paralyzing intrigues of jealous ambition and unscrupulous avarice, she will throw open wider and yet a wider door for thousands who are now looking with an anxious eye for some land of rest.

OUR COURTS OF justices are open equally to the stranger and the citizen for the redress of grievances, for the remedy of injuries, and for the punishment of crime.

OUR NUMEROUS AND well-attended schools attest our efforts and our desire for the improvement of our children. Our churches for the worship of our Creator, everywhere to be seen, bear testimony to our acknowledgment of His providence.

THE NATIVE AFRICAN bowing down with us before the altar of the living God, declares that from us, feeble as we are, the light of Christianity has gone forth, while upon that curse of curses, the slave trade, a deadly blight has fallen, as far as our influence extends.

THEREFORE, IN THE name of humanity, virtue, and religion, in the name of the great God, our common Creator, we appeal to the nations of Christendom, and earnestly and respectfully ask of them that they will regard us with the sympathy and friendly considerations to which the peculiarities of our condition entitles us, and to that comity which marks the friendly intercourse of civilized and independent communities.

WRITTEN BY HILARY Teage, the signers of the Declaration of Independence were twelve representatives to the Constitutional Convention which convened in Monrovia on July 5, 1847:

Montserrado County
Samuel Benedict
Hilary Teage
Elijah Johnson
John N. Lewis
Beverly R. W Johnson
J.B. Gripon

Grand Bassa County
John Day
Amos Herring
Anthony W. Gardiner
Ephraim Titler

Sinoe County
Jacob Prout
Richard E Murray

THE CONSTITUTION OF THE REPUBLIC OF LIBERIA

PREAMBLE

We the People of the Republic of Liberia:

Acknowledging our devout gratitude to God for our existence as a Free, Sovereign and Independent State, and relying on His Divine Guidance for our survival as a Nation;

Realizing from many experiences during the course of our national existence which culminated in the Revolution of April 12, 1980, when our Constitution of July 26, 1847 was suspended, that all of our people, irrespective of history, tradition, creed, or ethnic background are of one common body politic;

Exercising our natural, inherent and inalienable rights to establish a framework of government for the purpose of promoting unity, liberty, peace, stability, equality, justice and human rights under the rule of law, with opportunities for political, social, moral, spiritual and cultural advancement of our society, for ourselves and for our posterity; and

Having resolved to live in harmony, to practice fraternal love, tolerance and understanding as a people and being fully mindful of our obligation to promote African unity and international peace and cooperation,

Do hereby solemnly make, establish, proclaim, and publish this Constitution for the governance of the Republic of Liberia.

CHAPTER I

STRUCTURE OF THE STATE

Article 1

All power is inherent in the people. All free governments are instituted by their authority and for their benefit and they have the right to alter and reform the same when their safety and happiness so require. In order to ensure democratic government which responds to the wishes of the governed, the people shall have the right at such period, and in such manner as provided for under this Constitution, to cause their public servants to leave office and to fill vacancies by regular elections and appointments.

Article 2

This Constitution is the supreme and fundamental law of Liberia and its provisions shall have binding force and effect on all authorities and persons throughout the Republic.

Any laws, treaties, statutes, decrees, customs and regulations found to be inconsistent with it shall, to the extent of the inconsistency, be void and of no legal effect. The Supreme Court, pursuant to its power of judicial review, is empowered to declare any inconsistent laws unconstitutional.

Article 3

Liberia is a unitary sovereign state divided into counties for administrative purposes. The form of government is Republican with three separate coordinate branches: the Legislative, the Executive and Judiciary. Consistent with the principles of separation of powers and checks and balances, no person holding office in one of these branches shall hold office in or exercise any of the powers assigned to either of the other two branches except as otherwise provided in this Constitution; and no person holding office in one of the said branches shall serve on any autonomous public agency.

CHAPTER II

GENERAL PRINCIPLES OF NATIONAL POLICY

Article 4

The principles contained in this Chapter shall be fundamental in the governance of the Republic and shall serve as guidelines in the formulation of legislative, executive and administrative directives, policy-making and their execution.

Article 5

The Republic shall:

a) aim at strengthening the national integration and unity of the people of Liberia, regardless of ethnic, regional or other differences, into one body politic; and the Legislature shall enact laws promoting national unification and the encouragement of all citizens to participate in government;

b) preserve, protect and promote positive Liberian culture, ensuring that traditional values which are compatible with public policy and national progress are adopted and developed as an integral part of the growing needs of the Liberian society;

c) take steps, by appropriate legislation and executive orders, to eliminate sectionalism and tribalism, and such abuses of power as the misuse of government resources, nepotism and all other corrupt practices.

Article 6

The Republic shall, because of the vital role assigned to the individual citizen under this Constitution for the social, economic and political wellbeing of Liberia, provide equal access to educational opportunities and facilities for all citizens to the extent of available resources. Emphasis shall be placed on the mass education of the Liberian people and the elimination of illiteracy.

Article 7

The Republic shall, consistent with the principles of individual freedom and social justice enshrined in this Constitution, manage the national economy and the natural resources of Liberia in such manner as shall ensure the maximum feasible participation of Liberian citizens under conditions of equality as to advance the general welfare of the Liberian people and the economic development of Liberia.

Article 8

The Republic shall direct its policy towards ensuring for all citizens, without discrimination, opportunities for employment and livelihood under just and humane conditions, and towards promoting safety, health and welfare facilities in employment.

Article 9

The Republic shall encourage the promotion of bilateral and regional cooperation between and among Liberia and other nations and the formation and maintenance of regional organizations aimed at the cultural, social, political and economic development of the peoples of Africa and other nations of the world.

Article 10

The Republic shall ensure the publication and dissemination of this Constitution throughout the Republic and the teaching of its principles and provisions in all institutions of learning in Liberia.

CHAPTER III

FUNDAMENTAL RIGHTS

Article 11

a) All persons are born equally free and independent and have certain natural, inherent and inalienable rights, among which are the right of enjoying and defending life and liberty, of pursuing and maintaining and security of the person and of acquiring, possessing and protecting property, subject to such qualifications as provided for in this Constitution.

b) All persons, irrespective of ethnic background, race, sex, creed, place of origin or political opinion, are entitled to the fundamental rights and freedoms of the individual, subject to such qualifications as provided for in this Constitution.

c) All persons are equal before the law and are therefore entitled to the equal protection of the law.

Article 12

No person shall be held in slavery or forced labor within the Republic, nor shall any citizen of Liberia nor any person resident therein deal in slaves or subject any other person to forced labor, debt bondage or peonage; but labor reasonably required in consequence of a court sentence or order conforming to acceptable labor standards, service in the military, work or service which forms part of normal civil obligations or service exacted in cases of emergency or calamity threatening the life or well-being of the community shall not be deemed forced labor.

Article 13

a) Every person lawfully within the Republic shall have the right to move freely throughout Liberia, to reside in any part thereof and to leave therefrom subject however to the safeguarding of public security, public order, public health or morals or the rights and freedoms of others.

b) Every Liberian Citizen shall have the right to leave and to enter Liberia at any time. Liberian citizens and non-Liberian residents may be extradited to foreign country for prosecution of a criminal offense in accordance with the provisions of an extradition treaty or other reciprocal international agreements in force. Non-Liberian residents may be expelled from the Republic of Liberia for cause.

Article 14

All persons shall be entitled to freedom of thought, conscience and religion and no person shall be hindered in the enjoyment thereof except as may be required by law to protect public safety, order, health, or morals or the fundamental rights and freedoms of others. All persons who, in the practice of their religion, conduct themselves peaceably, not obstructing others and conforming to the standards set out herein, shall be entitled to the protection of the law. No religious denomination or sect shall have any exclusive privilege or preference over any other, but all shall be treated alike; and no religious tests shall be required for any civil or military office or for the exercise of any civil right. Consistent with the principle of separation of religion and state, the Republic shall establish no state religion.

Article 15

a) Every person shall have the right to freedom of expression, being fully responsible for the abuse thereof. This right shall not be curtailed, restricted or enjoined by government save during an emergency declared in accordance with this Constitution.

b) The right encompasses the right to hold opinions without interference and the right to knowledge. It includes freedom of speech and of the press, academic freedom to receive and impart knowledge and information and the right of libraries to make such knowledge available. It includes non-interference with the use of the mail, telephone and telegraph. It likewise includes the right to remain silent.

c) In pursuance of this right, there shall be no limitation on the public right to be informed about the government and its functionaries.

d) Access to state owned media shall not be denied because of any disagreement with or dislike of the ideas express. Denial of such access may be challenged in a court of competent jurisdiction.

e) This freedom may be limited only by judicial action in proceedings grounded in defamation or invasion of the rights of privacy and publicity or in the commercial aspect of expression in deception, false advertising and copyright infringement.

Article 16

No person shall be subjected to interference with his privacy of person, family, home or correspondence except by order of a court of competent jurisdiction.

Article 17

All persons, at all times, in an orderly and peaceable manner, shall have the right to assemble and consult upon the common good, to instruct their representatives, to petition the Government or other functionaries for the redress of grievances and associate fully with others or refuse to associate in political parties, trade unions and other organizations.

Article 18

All Liberian citizens shall have equal opportunity for work and employment regardless of sex, creed, religion, ethnic background, place of origin or political affiliation, and all shall be entitled to equal pay for equal work.

Article 19

No person other than members of the Armed Forces of Liberia or of the militia in active service shall be subject to military law, or made to suffer any pains or penalties by virtue of that law, or be tried by courts-martial.

Article 20

a) No person shall be deprived of life, liberty, security of the person, property, privilege or any other right except as the outcome of a hearing judgment consistent with the provisions laid down in this Constitution and in accordance with due process of law. Justice shall be done without sale, denial or delay; and in all cases not arising in courts not of record, under courts-martial and upon impeachment, the parties shall have the right to trial by jury.

b) The right of an appeal from a judgment, decree, decision or ruling of any court or administrative board or agency, except the Supreme Court, shall be held inviolable. The legislature shall prescribe rules and procedures for the easy, expeditious and inexpensive filing and hearing of an appeal.

Article 21

a) No person shall be made subject to any law or punishment which was not in effect at the time of commission of an offense, nor shall the Legislature enact any bill of attainder or ex post facto law.

b) No person shall be subject to search or seizure of his person or property, whether on a criminal charge or for any other purpose, unless upon warrant lawfully issued upon probable cause supported by a solemn oath or affirmation, specifically identifying the person or place to be searched and stating the object of the search; provided, however, that a search or seizure shall be permissible without a search warrant where the arresting authorities act during the commission of a crime or in hot pursuit of a person who has committed a crime.

c) Every person suspected or accused of committing a crime shall immediately upon arrest be informed in detail of the charges, of the right to remain silent and of the fact that any statement made could be used against him in a court of law. Such person shall be entitled to counsel at every stage of the investigation and shall have the right not to be interrogated except in the presence of counsel. Any admission or other statements made by the accused in the absence of such counsel shall be deemed inadmissible as evidence in a court of law.

d)(i) All accused persons shall be bailable upon their personal recognizance or by sufficient sureties, depending upon the gravity of the charge, unless charged for capital offenses or grave offenses as defined by law.

(ii) Excessive bail shall not be required, nor excessive fines imposed, nor excessive punishment inflicted.

e) No person charged, arrested, restricted, detained or otherwise held in confinement shall be subject to torture or inhumane treatment; nor shall any person except military personnel, be kept or confined in any military facility; nor shall any person be seized and kept among convicted prisoners or treated as a convict, unless such person first shall have been convicted of a crime in court of competent jurisdiction. The Legislature shall make it a criminal offense and provide for appropriate penalties against any police or security officer, prosecutor, administrator or any other public or security officer, prosecutor, administrator or any other public official acting in contravention of this provision; and any person so damaged by the conduct of any such public official shall have a civil remedy therefor, exclusive of any criminal penalties imposed.

f) Every person arrested or detained shall be formally charged and presented before a court of competent jurisdiction within forty-eight hours. Should the court determine the existence of a prima facie case against the accused, it shall issue a formal writ of arrest setting out the charge or charges and shall provide for a speedy trial. There shall be no preventive detention.

g) The right to the writ of habeas corpus, being essential to the protection of human rights, shall be guaranteed at all times, and any person arrested or detained and not presented to court within the period specified may in consequence exercise this right.

h) No person shall be held to answer for a capital or infamous crime except in cases of impeachment, cases arising in the Armed Forces and petty offenses, unless upon indictment by Grand Jury; and in all such cases, the accused shall have the right to a speedy, public and impartial trial by a jury of the vicinity, unless such person shall, with appropriate understanding, expressly waive the right to a jury trial. In all criminal cases, the accused shall have the right to be represented by counsel of his choice, to confront witnesses against him and to have compulsory process for obtaining witnesses in his favor. He shall not be compelled to furnish evidence against himself and he shall be presumed innocent until the contrary is proved beyond a reasonable doubt. No person shall be subject to double jeopardy.

i) The right to counsel and the rights of counsel shall be inviolable. There shall be no interference with the lawyer-client relationship. In all trials, hearings, interrogatories and other proceedings where a person is accused of a criminal offense, the accused shall have the right to counsel of his choice; and where the accused is unable to secure such representation, the Republic shall make available legal aid services to ensure the protection of his rights.

There shall be absolute immunity from any government sanctions or interference in the performance of legal services as a counselor or advocate; lawyers' offices and homes shall not be searched or papers examined or taken save pursuant to a search warrant and court order; and no lawyer shall be prevented from or punished for providing legal services, regardless of the charges against or the guilt of his client, no lawyer shall be barred from practice for political reasons.

j) Any person who, upon conviction of a criminal offense, was deprived of the enjoyment of his civil rights and liberties, shall have the same automatically restored upon serving the sentence and satisfying any other penalty imposed, or upon an executive pardon.

Article 22

a) Every person shall have the right to own property alone as well as in association with others; provided that only Liberian citizens shall have the right to own real property within the Republic.

b) Private property rights, however, shall not extend to any mineral resources on or beneath any land or to any lands under the seas and waterways of the Republic. All mineral resources in and under the seas and other waterways shall belong to the Republic and be used by and for the entire Republic.

c) Non-citizen missionary, educational and other benevolent institutions shall have the right to own property, as long as that property is used for the purposes for which acquired; property no longer so used shall escheat to the Republic)

d) The Republic may, on the basis of reciprocity, convey to a foreign government property to be used perpetually for its diplomatic activities. This land shall not be transferred or otherwise conveyed to any other party or used for any other purpose, except upon the expressed permission of the Government of Liberia. All property so conveyed may escheat to the Republic in the event of a cessation of diplomatic relations.

Article 23

a) The property which a person possesses at the time of marriage or which may afterwards be acquired as a result of one's own labors shall not be held for or otherwise applied to the liquidation of the debts or other obligations of the spouse, whether contracted before or after marriage; nor shall the property which by law is to be secured to a man or a woman be alienated or be controlled by that person's spouse save by free and voluntary consent.

b) The Legislature shall enact laws to govern the devolution of estates and establish rights of inheritance and descent for spouses of both statutory and customary marriages so as to give adequate protection to surviving spouses and children of such marriages.

Article 24

a) While the inviolability of private property shall be guaranteed by the Republic, expropriation may be authorized for the security of the nation in the event of armed conflict or where the public health and safety are endangered or for any other public purposes, provided:

(i) that reasons for such expropriation are given;

(ii) that there is prompt payment of just compensation;

(iii) that such expropriation or the compensation offered may be challenged freely by the owner of the property in a court of law with no penalty for having brought such action; and

(iv) that when property taken for public use ceases to be so used, the Republic shall accord the former owner or those entitled to the property through such owner, the right of first refusal to reacquire the property.

b) All real property held by a person whose certificate of naturalization has been cancelled shall escheat to the Republic, unless such person shall have a spouse and/or lineal heirs who are Liberian citizens, in which case the real property shall be transferred to them in accordance with the intestacy law.

c) The power of the Legislature to provide punishment for treason or other crimes shall not include a deprivation or forfeiture of the right of inheritance, although its enjoyment by the convicted person shall be postponed during a term of imprisonment judicially imposed; provided that if the convicted person has minor children and a spouse, the spouse or next of kin in the order of priority shall administer the same. No punishment shall preclude the inheritance, enjoyment or forfeiture by others entitled thereto of any property which the convicted person at the time of conviction or subsequent thereto may have possessed.

Article 25

Obligation of contract shall be guaranteed by the Republic and no laws shall be passed which might impair this right.

Article 26

Where any person or any association alleges that any of the rights granted under this Constitution or any legislation or directives are constitutionally contravened, that person or association may invoke the privilege and benefit of court direction, order or writ, including a judgment of unconstitutionality; and anyone injured by an act of the Government or any person acting under its authority, whether in property, contract, tort or otherwise, shall have the right to bring suit for appropriate redress. All such suits brought against the Government shall originate in a Claims Court; appeals from judgment of the Claims Court shall lie directly to the Supreme Court.

CHAPTER IV

CITIZENSHIP

Article 27

a) All persons who, on the coming into force of this Constitution were lawfully citizens of Liberia shall continue to be Liberian citizens.

b) In order to preserve, foster and maintain the positive Liberian culture, values and character, only persons who are Negroes or of Negro descent shall qualify by birth or by naturalization to be citizens of Liberia.

c) The Legislature shall, adhering to the above standard, prescribe such other qualification criteria for the procedures by which naturalization may be obtained.

Article 28

Any person, at least one of whose parents was a citizen of Liberia at the time of the Person's birth, shall be a citizen of Liberia; provided that any such person shall upon reaching maturity renounce any other citizenship acquired by virtue of one parent being a citizen of another country. No citizen of the Republic shall be deprived of citizenship or nationality except as provided by law; and no person shall be denied the right to change citizenship or nationality.

CHAPTER V

THE LEGISLATURE

Article 29

The legislative power of the Republic shall be vested in the Legislature of Liberia which shall consist of two separate houses: A Senate and a House of Representatives, both of which must pass on all legislation. The enacting style shall be: "It is enacted by the Senate and House of Representatives of the Republic of Liberia in Legislature assembled."

Article 30

Citizens of Liberia who meet the following qualifications are eligible to become members of the Legislature.

a) for the Senate, have attained the age of 30 years and for the House of Representatives, have attained the age of 25 years;

b) be domiciled in the country or constituency to be represented not less than one year prior to the time of the election and be a taxpayer.

Article 31

Each member of the Legislature, before taking his seat and entering upon the duties of office, shall take and subscribe to a solemn oath of affirmation, before the presiding officer of the House to which such person was elected and in the presence of other members of that House, to uphold and defend the Constitution and laws of the Republic and to discharge faithfully the duties of such office.

Article 32

a) The Legislature shall assemble in regular session once a year on the second working Monday in January.

b) The President shall, on his own initiative or upon receipt of a certificate signed by at least one-fourth of the total membership of each House, and by proclamation, extend a regular session of the Legislature beyond the date for adjournment or call a special extraordinary session of that body to discuss or act upon matters of national emergency and concern. When the extension or call is at the request of the Legislature, the proclamation shall be issued not later than forty-eight hours after receipt of the certificate by the President.

Article 33

Simple majority of each House shall constitute a quorum for the transaction of business, but a lower number may adjourn from day to day and compel the attendance of absent members. Whenever the House of Representatives and the Senate shall meet in joint session, the presiding officer of the House of Representatives shall preside.

Article 34

The Legislature shall have the power:

a) to create new counties and other political sub-division, and readjust existing county boundaries;

b) to provide for the security of the Republic;

c) to provide for the common defense, to declare war and authorize the Executive to conclude peace; to raise and support the Armed Forces of the Republic, and to make appropriations therefor provided that no appropriation of money for that use shall be for a longer term than on year; and to make rules for the governance of the Armed Forces of the Republic;

d) to levy taxes, duties, imports, exercise and other revenues, to borrow money, issue currency, mint coins, and to make appropriations for the fiscal governance of the Republic, subject to the following qualifications:

(i) All revenue bills, whether subsidies, charges, imports, duties or taxes, and other financial bills, shall originate in the House of Representatives, but the Senate may propose or concur with amendments as on other bills. No other financial charge shall be established, fixed, laid or levied on any individual, community or locality under any pretext whatsoever except by the expressed consent of the individual, community or locality. In all such cases, a true and correct account of funds collected shall be made to the community or locality;

(ii) no monies shall be drawn from the treasure except in consequence of appropriations made by legislative enactment and upon warrant of the President; and no coin shall be minted or national currency issued except by the expressed authority of the Legislature. An annual statement and account of the expenditure of all public monies shall be submitted by the office of the President to the Legislature and published once a year;

(iii) no loans shall be raised by the Government on behalf of the Republic or guarantees given for any public institutions or authority otherwise than by or under the authority of a legislative enactment;

e) to constitute courts inferior to the Supreme Court, including circuit courts, claims courts and such courts with prescribed jurisdictional powers as may be deemed necessary for the proper administration of justice throughout the Republic;

f) to approve treaties, conventions and such other international agreements negotiated or signed on behalf of the Republic;

g) to regulate trade and commence between Liberia and other nations;

h) to establish laws for citizenship, naturalization and residence;

i) to enact the election laws;

j) to establish various categories of criminal offenses and provide for the punishment thereof;

k) to enact laws providing pension scheme for various categories of government officials and employees in accordance with age and tenure of service; and

l) to make other laws which shall be necessary and proper for carrying into execution the foregoing powers, and all other powers vested by this Constitution in the Government of the Republic, or in any department or officer thereof.

Article 35

Each bill or resolution which shall have passed both Houses of the Legislature shall, before it becomes law, be laid before the President for his approval. If he grants approval, it shall become law. If the President does not approve such bill or resolution, he shall return it, with his objections, to the House in which it originated. In so doing, the President may disapprove of the entire bill or resolution or any item or items thereof. This veto may be overridden by the re-passage of such bill, resolution or item thereof by a veto of two-thirds of the members in each House, in which case it shall become law. If the

President does not return the bill or resolution within twenty days after the same shall have been laid before him it shall become law in like manner as if he had signed it, unless the Legislature by adjournment prevents its return.

No bill or resolution shall embrace more than one subject which shall be expressed in its title.

Article 36

The Senators and Representatives shall receive from the Republic remuneration for their services to be fixed by law, provided that any increase shall become effective at the beginning of the next fiscal year.

Article 37

In the event of a vacancy in the Legislature caused by death, resignation, expulsion or otherwise, the presiding officer shall within 30 days notify the Elections Commission thereof. The Elections Commission shall not later than 90 days thereafter cause a by-election to be held; provided that where such vacancy occurs within 90 days prior to the holding of general elections, the filling of the vacancy shall await the holding of such general elections.

Article 38

Each House shall adopt its own rules of procedure, enforce order and with the concurrence of two-thirds of the entire membership, may expel a member for cause. Each House shall establish its own committees and sub-committees; provided, however, that the committees on revenues and appropriations shall consist of one member from each County. All rules adopted by the Legislature shall conform to the requirements of due process of law laid down in this Constitution.

Article 39

The Legislature shall cause a census of the Republic to be undertaken every ten years.

Article 40

Neither House shall adjourn for more than five days without the consent of the other and both Houses shall always sit in the same city.

Article 41

The business of the Legislature shall be concluded in the English language or, when adequate preparations shall have been made, in one more of the languages of the Republic as the Legislature may by resolution approve.

Article 42

No member of the Senate or House of Representatives shall be arrested, detained, prosecuted or tried as a result of opinions expressed or votes cast in the exercise of the functions of his office. Members shall be privileged from arrest while attending, going to or returning from sessions of the Legislature, except for treason, felony or breach of the peace. All official acts done or performed and all statement made in the Chambers of the Legislature shall be privileged, and no Legislator shall be held accountable or punished therefor.

Article 43

The power to prepare a bill of impeachment is vested solely in the House of Representatives, and the power to try all impeachments is vested solely in the Senate. When the President, Vice President or an Associate Justice is to be tried, the Chief Justice shall preside; when the Chief Justice or a judge of a subordinate court of record is to be tried, the President of the Senate shall preside. No person shall be impeached but by the concurrence of two-thirds of the total membership of the Senate. Judgments in such cases shall not extend beyond removal from office and disqualification to hold public office in the Republic; but the party may be tried at law for the same offense. The Legislature shall prescribe the procedure for impeachment proceedings which shall be in conformity with the requirements of due process of law.

Article 44

Contempt of the Legislature shall consist of actions which obstruct the legislative functions or which obstruct or impede members or officers of the Legislature in the discharge of their legislative duties and may be punished by the House concerned by reasonable sanctions after a hearing consistent with due process of law. No sanctions shall extend beyond the session of the Legislature wherein it is imposed, and any sanction imposed shall conform to the provisions on Fundamental Rights laid down in the Constitution. Disputes between legislators and non-members which are properly cognizable in the courts shall not be entertained or heard in the Legislature.

Article 45

The Senate shall be composed of Senators elected for a term of nine years by the registered voters in each of the counties, but a Senator elected in a by-election to fill a vacancy created by death, resignation, expulsion or otherwise, shall be so elected to serve only the remainder of the unexpired term of office. Each county shall elect two Senators and each Senator shall have one vote in the Senate. Senators shall be eligible for re-election.

Article 46

Immediately after the Senate shall have assembled following the elections prior to the coming into force of this Constitution, the Senators shall be divided into two categories as a result of the votes cast in each county. The Senator with the higher votes cast shall be the Senator from a county shall be placed in the same category. The seats of Senators of the first category shall be vacated at the expiration of the ninth year. In the interest of legislative continuity, the Senators of the second category shall serve a first term of six years only, after the first elections. Thereafter, all Senators shall be elected to serve a term of nine years.

Article 47

The Senate shall elect once every six years a President Pro Tempore who shall preside in the absence of the President of the Senate, and such shall officers as shall ensure the proper functioning of the Senate. The President Pro Tempore and other officers so elected may be removed from office for cause by resolution of a two-thirds majority of the members of the Senate.

Article 48

The House of Representatives shall be composed of members elected for a term of six years by the registered voters in each of the legislative constituencies of the counties, but a member of the House of Representatives elected in a by-election to fill a vacancy created by death, resignation or otherwise, shall be elected to serve only the remainder of the unexpired term of the office. Members of the House of Representatives shall be eligible for re-election.

Article 49

The House of Representative shall elect once every six years a Speaker who shall be the presiding officer of that body, a Deputy Speaker, and such other officers as shall ensure the proper functioning of the House. The Speaker, the Deputy Speaker and other officers so elected may be removed from office for cause by resolution of a two-thirds majority of the members of the House.

CHAPTER VI

THE EXECUTIVE

Article 50

The Executive Power of the Republic shall be vested in the President who shall be Head of State, Head of Government and Commander-in-Chief of the Armed Forces of Liberia. The President shall be elected by universal adult suffrage of registered voters in the Republic and shall hold office for a term of six years commencing at noon on the third working Monday in January of the year immediately following the elections. No person shall serve as President for more than two terms.

Article 51

There shall be a Vice–President who shall assist the President in the discharge of his functions. The Vice–President shall be elected on the same political ticket and shall serve the same term as the President. The Vice–President shall be President of the Senate and preside over its deliberations without the right to vote, except in the case of a tie vote. He shall attend meetings of the cabinet and other governmental meetings and shall perform such functions as the President shall delegate or deem appropriate; provided that no powers specifically vested in the President by the provisions of this Constitution shall be delegated to the Vice–President.

Article 52

No person shall be eligible to hold the office of President or Vice–President, unless that person is:

a) a natural born Liberian citizen of not less than 35 years of age:

b) the owner of unencumbered real property valued at not less than twenty-five thousand dollars; and

c) resident in the Republic ten years prior to his election, provided that the President and the Vice–President shall not come from the same County.

Article 53

a) The President and the Vice–President shall, before entering on the execution of the duties of their respective offices, take a solemn oath or affirmation to preserve, protect and defend the Constitution and laws of the Republic and faithfully execute the duties of the office. The oath or affirmation shall be administered in joint convention of both Houses of the Legislature by the Chief Justice or, in his absence, the most senior Associate Justice.

b) In an emergency where the Chief Justice and the Associate Justice are not available, such oath or affirmation shall be administered by a judge of a subordinate court of record.

Article 54

The President shall nominate and, with the consent of the Senate, appoint and commission

a) Cabinet ministers, deputy and assistant cabinet ministers;

b) Ambassadors, ministers, consuls; and

c) The Chief Justice and Associate Justice of the Supreme Court and judges of subordinate courts;

d) Superintendents, other county officials and officials of other political sub-divisions;

e) Members of the military from the rank of lieutenant of its equivalent and above; and

f) Marshals, deputy marshals, and sheriffs.

Article 55

The President shall appoint and commission Notaries Public and Justices of the Peace who shall hold office for a term of two years but may be removed by the President for cause. They shall be eligible for appointment.

Article 56

a) All cabinet ministers, deputy and assistant cabinet ministers, ambassadors, ministers and consuls, superintendents of counties and other government officials, both military and civilian, appointed by the President pursuant to this Constitution shall hold their offices at the pleasure of the President.

b) There shall be elections of Paramount, Clan and Town Chiefs by the registered voters in their respective localities, to serve for a term of six years. They may be re-elected and may be removed only by the President for proved misconduct. The Legislature shall enact laws to provide for their qualifications as may be required.

Article 57

The President shall have the power to conduct the foreign affairs of the Republic and in that connection he is empowered to conclude treaties, conventions and similar international agreements with the concurrence of a majority of each House of the Legislature.

Article 58

The President shall, on the fourth working Monday in January of each year, present the administration's legislative program for the ensuing session, and shall once a year report to the Legislature on the state of the Republic. In presenting the economic condition of the Republic, the report shall cover expenditure as well as income.

Article 59

The President may remit any public forfeitures and penalties suspend any fines and sentences, grant reprieves and pardons, and restore civil rights after conviction for all public offenses, except impeachment.

Article 60

The President and the Vice–President shall receive salaries which shall be determined by the Legislature and be paid by the Republic. Such salaries shall be subject to taxes as defined by law and shall neither be increased nor diminished during the period for which the President and the Vice–President shall have been elected.

Article 61

The President shall be immune from any suits, actions or proceedings, judicial or otherwise, and from arrest, detention or other actions on account of any act done by him while President of Liberia pursuant to any provision of this Constitution or any other laws of the Republic. The President shall not, however, be immune from prosecution upon removal from office for the commission of any criminal act done while President.

Article 62

The President and the Vice–President may be removed from office by impeachment for treason, bribery and other felonies, violation of the Constitution or gross misconduct.

Article 63

a) Whenever a person elected to the office of President dies or is otherwise incapacitated before being inaugurated into office, the Vice–President elected shall succeed to the office of President, and this accession shall commence a term.

b) Whenever the office of the President shall become vacant by reason of death, resignation, impeachment, or the President shall be declared incapable of carrying out the duties and functions of his office, the Vice–President shall succeed to the of the President to complete the unexpired term. In such a case, this not constitute a term.

c) The Legislature shall, no later than one year after the coming into force of this Constitution, prescribe the guidelines and determine the procedure under which the President, by reason of illness, shall be declared incapable of carrying out the functions of his office.

d) Whenever the office of the Vice–President becomes vacant by reason of death, resignation, impeachment, inability or otherwise, the President shall, without delay, nominate a candidate who, with the concurrence of both Houses of the Legislature, shall be sworn in and hold office as Vice–President until the next general elections are held. Whenever the Vice–President elect dies, resigns, or is incapacitated before being inaugurated, the President elected on the same ticket with him, shall, after being inaugurated into office, nominate without delay a candidate who, with the concurrence of both Houses of the Legislature, shall be sworn in and hold office as Vice–President until the next general elections are held.

Article 64

Whenever the office of the President and of the Vice–President shall become vacant by reason of removal, death, resignation, inability or other disability of the President and Vice–President, the Speaker of the House of Representatives shall be sworn in as Acting President until the holding of elections to fill the vacancies so created. Should the Speaker be legally incapable or otherwise unable to assume the office of Acting President, then the same shall devolve upon the President Pro Tempore of the Senate. In any further line of descent, the office shall devolve in order upon the Deputy Speaker and members of the Cabinet in the order of precedence as established by law. The Elections Commission shall within ninety days conduct elections for a new President and a new Vice–President.

CHAPTER VII

THE JUDICIARY

Article 65

The Judicial Power of the Republic shall be vested in a Supreme Court and such subordinate courts as the legislature may from time to time establish. The courts shall apply both statutory and customary laws in accordance with the standards enacted by the Legislature. Judgments of the Supreme Court shall be final and binding and shall not be subject to appeal or review by any other branch of Government. Nothing in this Article shall prohibit administrative consideration of the justiciable matter prior to review by a court of competent jurisdiction.

Article 66

The Supreme Court shall be the final arbiter of constitutional issues and shall exercise final appellate jurisdiction in all cases, whether emanating from courts of record, courts not of record, administrative agencies, autonomous agencies or any other authority, both as to law and fact except cases involving ambassadors, ministers, or cases in which a country is a party. In all such cases, the Supreme Court shall exercise original jurisdiction. The Legislature shall make no law nor create any exceptions as would deprive the Supreme Court of any of the powers granted herein.

Article 67

The Supreme Court shall comprise of one Chief Justice and four Associate Justice, a majority of whom shall be deemed competent to transact the business of the Court. It a quorum is not obtained to enable the Court to hear any case, a circuit judge in the order of seniority shall sit as an ad hoc justice of the Supreme Court.

Article 68

The Chief Justice and Associate Justice of the Supreme Court shall, with the consent of the Senate, be appointed and commissioned by the President; provided that any person so appointed shall be:

a) a citizen of Liberia and of good moral character; and

b) a counselor of the Supreme Court Bar who has practiced for at least 5 years.

Article 69

The judges of subordinate courts of record shall, with the consent of the Senate, be appointed and commissioned by the President, provided that any person so appointed shall be:

a) a citizen of Liberia and of good moral character; and

b) an Attorney-at-Law who has practiced for at least 3 years, or a counselor of the Supreme Court Bar.

Article 70

The Chief Justice and the Associate Justices of the Supreme Court and all judges of subordinate courts shall, before assuming the functions of their office, subscribe to a solemn oath or affirmation to discharge faithfully and impartially the duties and functions of their office and to preserve, protect and defend the Constitution and laws of the Republic. The oath or affirmation shall be administered by the president or his designee.

Article 71

The Chief Justice and Associates Justices of the Supreme Court and the judges of subordinate courts of record shall hold office during good behavior. They may be removed upon impeachment and conviction by the Legislature based on proved misconduct, gross breach of duty, inability to perform the functions of their office, or conviction in a court of law for treason, bribery or other infamous crimes.

Article 72

a) The Justices of the Supreme Court and all other judges shall receive such salaries, allowances and benefits as shall be established by law. Such salaries shall be subject to taxes as defined by law, provided that they shall not otherwise be diminished. Allowances and benefits paid to Justices of the Supreme Court and judges of subordinate courts may by law be increased but may not be diminished except under a national program enacted by the Legislature; nor shall such allowance and benefits be subject to taxation.

b) The Chief Justice and the Associate Justices of the Supreme Court and judges of subordinate courts of record shall be retired at the age of seventy; provided, however, that a justice of judge who has attained that age may continue in office for as long as may be necessary to enable him to render judgment or perform any other judicial duty in regard to proceedings entertained by him before the attained that age.

Article 73

No judicial official shall be summoned, arrested, detained, prosecuted or tried civilly or criminally by or at the instance of any person or authority on account of judicial opinions rendered or expressed, judicial statements made and judicial acts done in the course of a trial in open court or in chambers, except for treason or other felonies, misdemeanor or breach of the peace. Statements made and acts done by such officials in the course of a judicial proceeding shall be privileged, and, subject to the above qualification, no such statement made or acts done shall be admissible into evidence against them at any trial or proceeding.

Article 74

In all matters of contempt of court, whether in the Supreme Court or in other courts, the penalties to be imposed shall be fixed by the Legislature and shall conform to the provision on Fundamental Rights laid down in this Constitution.

Article 75

The Supreme Court shall from time to time make rules of court for the purpose of regulating the practice, procedures and manner by which cases shall be commenced and heard before it and all other subordinate courts. It shall prescribe such code of conduct for lawyers appearing before it and all other subordinate courts as may be necessary to facilitate the proper discharge of the court's functions. Such rules and code, however, shall not contravene any statutory provisions or any provisions of this Constitution.

Article 76

a) Treason against the Republic shall consist of:

(1) levying war against the Republic;

(2) aligning oneself with or aiding and abetting another nation or people with whom Liberia is at war or in a state of war;

(3) acts of espionage for an enemy state;

(4) attempting by overt act to overthrow the Government, rebellion against the Republic, insurrection and mutiny; and

(5) abrogating or attempting to abrogate, subverting or attempting or conspiring to subvert the Constitution by use of force or show of force or any other means which attempts to undermine this Constitution.

The Legislature shall have the power to declare the punishment for treason; provided, however, that such punishment shall not include a deprivation or forfeiture of the right of inheritance by the convicted person of any property although he may not be entitled to enjoyment thereof for as long as he continues to serve the term of imprisonment imposed after conviction in a court of competent jurisdiction. The right to enjoyment of any property inherited or otherwise conveyed to or acquired by such convicted person shall be automatically restored upon serving the term of imprisonment or other punishment, or upon an executive pardon by the President. No punishment shall preclude the inheritance and enjoyment, or cause the forfeiture by others entitled thereto, of any property which the convicted person at the time of any conviction or subsequent thereto may have possessed or been seized.

CHAPTER VIII

POLITICAL PARTIES AND ELECTIONS

Article 77

a) Since the essence of democracy is free competition of ideas expressed by political parties and political groups as well as by individuals, parties may freely be established to advocate the political opinions of the people. Laws, regulations, decrees or measures which might have the effect of creating a one-party state shall be declared unconstitutional.

b) All elections shall be by secret ballot as may be determined by the Elections Commission, and every Liberian citizen not less than 18 years of age, shall have the right to be registered as a voter and to vote in public elections and referenda under this Constitution. The Legislature shall enact laws indicating the category of Liberians who shall not form or become members of political parties.

Article 78

As used in this Chapter, unless the context otherwise requires, an "association" means a body of persons, corporate or other, which acts together for a common purpose, and includes a group of people organized for any ethnic, social, cultural, occupational or religious objectives; a "political party" shall be an association with a membership of not less than five hundred qualified voters in each of at least six counties, whose activities include canvassing for votes on any public issue or in support of a candidate for elective public office; and an "independent candidate" shall be a person seeking electoral post or office with or without his own organization, acting independently of a political party.

Article 79

No association, by whatever name called, shall function as a political party, nor shall any citizen be an independent candidate for election to public office, unless:

a) The association or independent candidate and his organization meet the minimum registration requirements laid down by the Elections Commission and are registered with it. Registration requirements shall include filing with the Elections Commission a copy of the constitution of the association and guidelines of the independent candidate and his organization, a detailed statement of the names and addresses of the association and its officers or of the independent candidate and the officers of his organization, and fulfillment of the provision of sub-sections (b), (c), (d) and (e) hereof. Registration by the Elections Commission of any association or independent candidate and his organization shall vest in the entity or candidate and his organization so registered legal personality, with the capacity to own property, real, personal or mixed, to sue and be sued and to hold accounts. A denial of registration or failure by the Elections Commission to register any applicant may be challenged by the applicant in the Supreme Court;

b) the membership of the association or the independent candidate's organization is open to every citizen of Liberia, irrespective of sex, religion or ethnic background, except as otherwise provided in this Constitution.

c) the headquarters of the association or independent candidate and his organization is situated:

(i) in the capital of the Republic where an association is involved or where an independent candidate seeks election to the office of President or Vice–President;

(ii) in the headquarters of the county where an independent candidate seeks election as a Senator; and

(iii) in the electoral center in the constituency where the candidate seeks election as a member of the House of Representatives or to any other public office;

d) the name, objective, emblem or motto of the association or of the independent candidate and his organization is free from any religious connotations or divisive ethnic implications and that the activities of the association or independent candidate are not limited to a special group or, in the case of an association, limited to a particular geographic area of Liberia;

e) the constitution and rules of the political party shall conform to the provisions of this Constitution, provide for the democratic elections of officers and/or governing body at least once every six years, and ensure the election of officers from as many of the regions and ethnic groupings in the country as possible. All amendments to the Constitution or rules of a political party shall be registered with the Elections Commission no later than ten days from the effective dates of such amendments.

Article 80

a) Parties or organizations which, by reason of their aims or the behavior of their adherents, seek to impair or abolish the free democratic society of Liberia or to endanger the existence of the Republic shall be denied registration.

b) Parties or organization which retain, organize, train or equip any person or group of persons for the use or display of physical force or coercion in promoting any political objective or interest, trained or equipped, shall be denied registration, or if registered, shall have their registration revoked.

c) Every Liberian citizen shall have the right to be registered in a constituency, and to vote in public elections only in the constituency where registered, either in person or by absentee ballot; provided that such citizen shall have the right to change his voting constituency as may be prescribed by the Legislature.

d) Each constituency shall have an approximately equal population of 20,000, or such number of citizens as the legislature shall prescribe in keeping with population growth and movements as revealed by a national census; provided that the total number of electoral constituencies in the Republic shall not exceed one hundred.

e) Immediately following a national census and before the next election, the Elections Commission shall reapportion the constituencies in accordance with the new population figures so that every constituency shall have as close to the same population as possible; provided, however, that a constituency must be solely within a county.

Article 81

Any citizen, political party, organization, or association, being resident in Liberia, of Liberian nationality or origin and not otherwise disqualified under the provisions of this Constitution and laws of the land, shall have the right to canvass for the votes for any political party or candidate at any election, provided that corporate and business organizations and labor unions are excluded from so canvassing directly or indirectly in whatsoever form.

Article 82

a) Any citizen or citizens, political party association or organization, being of Liberian nationality or origin, shall have the right to contribute to the funds or election expenses of any political party or candidate; provided that corporate and business organizations and labor unions shall be excluded from making and contribution to the funds or expenses of any political party. The Legislature shall by law prescribe the guidelines under which such contributions may be made and the maximum amount which may be contributed.

b) No political party or organization may hold or possess any funds or other assets outside of Liberia; nor may they or any independent candidates retain any funds or assets remitted or sent to them from outside Liberia unless remitted or sent by Liberian citizens residing abroad. Any funds or other assets received directly or indirectly in contravention of this restriction shall be paid over or transferred to the Elections Commission within twenty-one days of receipt. Information on all funds received from abroad shall be filed promptly with the Elections Commission.

c) The Elections Commission shall have the power to examine into and order certified audits of the financial transactions of political parties and independent candidates and their organizations. The Commission shall prescribe the kinds of records to be kept and the manner in which they shall be conducted by a certified chartered public accountant, not a member of any political party.

Article 83

a) Voting for the President, Vice–President, members of the Senate and members of the House of Representatives shall be conducted throughout the Republic on the second Tuesday in October of each election year.

b) All elections of public officers shall be determined by an absolute majority of the votes cast. If no candidate obtains an absolute majority in the first ballot, a second ballot shall be conducted on the second Tuesday following. The two candidates who received the greatest numbers of votes on the first ballot shall be designated to participate in the run-off election.

c) The returns of the elections shall be declared by the Elections Commission not later than fifteen days after the casting of ballots. Any party or candidate who complains about the manner in which the elections were conducted or who challenges the results thereof shall have the right to file a complaint with the Elections Commission. Such complaint must be filed not later than seven days after the announcement of the results of the elections.

The Elections Commission shall, within thirty days of receipt of the complaint, conduct an impartial investigation and render a decision which may involve a dismissal of the complaint or a nullification of the election of a candidate. Any political party or independent candidate affected by such decision shall not later than seven days appeal against it to the Supreme Court.

The Elections Commission shall within seven days of receipt of the notice of appeal, forward all the records in the case to the Supreme Court, which not later than seven days thereafter, shall hear and make its determination. If the Supreme Court nullifies or sustains the nullification of the election of any candidate, for whatever reasons, the Elections commission shall within sixty days of the decision of the Court conduct new elections to fill the vacancy. If the court sustains the election of a candidate, the Elections Commission shall act to effectuate the mandate of the Court.

d) Every political party shall, on September 1 of each year, and every candidate of such political party and every independent candidate shall, not later than thirty days prior to the holding of an election in which he is a candidate, publish and submit to the Elections Commission detailed statements of assets and liabilities. These shall include the enumeration of sources of funds and other assets, plus lists of expenditures. Where the filing of such statements is made in an election year, every political party and independent candidate shall be required to file with the Elections Commissions additional detailed supplementary statements of all funds received and expenditures made by them from the date of filing of the original statements to the date of the elections. Any political party or independent candidate who ceases to function shall publish and submit a final financial statement to the Elections Commission.

Article 84

The Legislature shall by law provide penalties for any violations of the relevant provisions of this Chapter, and shall enact laws and regulations in furtherance thereof not later than 1986; provided that such penalties, laws or regulations shall not be inconsistent with any provisions of this Constitution.

CHAPTER IX

EMERGENCY POWERS

Article 85

The President, as Commander-in-Chief of the Armed Forces, may order any portion of the Armed Forces into a state of combat readiness in defense of the Republic, before or after the declaration of a state of emergency, as may be warranted by the situation. All military power or authority shall at all times, however, be held in subordination to the civil authority and the Constitution.

Article 86

a) The President may, in consultation with the Speaker of the House of Representatives and the President Pro Tempore of the Senate, proclaim and declare and the existence of a state of emergency in the Republic or any part thereof. Acting pursuant thereto, the President may suspend or affect certain rights, freedoms and guarantees contained in this Constitution and exercise such other emergency powers as may be necessary and appropriate to take care of the emergency, subject, however, to the limitations contained in this Chapter.

b) A state of emergency may be declared only where there is a threat or outbreak of war or where there is civil unrest affecting the existence, security or well-being of the Republic amounting to a clear and present danger.

Article 87

a) Emergency powers do not include the power to suspend or abrogate the Constitution, dissolve the Legislature, or suspend or dismiss the Judiciary; and no constitutionals amendment shall be promulgated during a state of emergency. Where the Legislature is not in session, it must be convened immediately in special session and remain in session during the entire period of the state of emergency.

b) The writ of habeas corpus shall remain available and exercisable at all times and shall not be suspended on account of any state of emergency. It shall be enjoyed in the freest, easy, inexpensive, expeditious and ample manner. Any person who suffers from a violation of this right may challenge such violation in a court of competent jurisdiction.

Article 88

The President shall, immediately upon the declaration of a state of emergency, but not later than seven days thereafter, lay before the Legislature at its regular session or at a specially convened session, the facts and circumstances leading to such declaration. The Legislature shall within seventy-two hours, by joint resolution voted by two-thirds of the membership of each house, decide whether the proclamation of a state of emergency is justified or whether the measures taken thereunder are appropriate. If the two-thirds vote is not obtained, the emergency automatically shall be revoked. Where the Legislature shall deem it necessary to revoke the state of emergency or to modify the measures taken thereunder, the President shall act accordingly and immediately carry out the decisions of the Legislature.

CHAPTER X

AUTONOMOUS PUBLIC COMMISSIONS

Article 89

The following Autonomous Public Commissions are hereby established:

A. CIVIL SERVICE COMMISSION;

B. ELECTIONS COMMISSION; and

C. GENERAL AUDITING COMMISSION

The Legislature shall enact laws for the governance of these Commissions and create other agencies as may be necessary for the effective operation of Government.

CHAPTER XI

MISCELLANEOUS

Article 90

a) No person, whether elected or appointed to any public office, shall engage in any other activity which shall be against public policy, or constitute conflict of interest.

b) No person holding office shall demand and receive any other perquisites, emoluments or benefits, directly or indirectly, on account of any duty required by Government.

c) The Legislature shall, in pursuance of the above provision, prescribe a Code of Conduct for all public officials and employees, stipulating the acts which constitute conflict of interest or are against public policy, and the penalties for violation thereof.

CHAPTER XII

AMENDMENTS

Article 91

This Constitution may be amended whenever a proposal by either (1) two-thirds of the membership of both Houses of the Legislature or (2) a petition submitted to the Legislature, by not fewer than 10,000 citizens which receives the concurrence of two-thirds of the membership of both Houses of the Legislature, is ratified by two-thirds of the registered voters, voting in a referendum conducted by the Elections Commission not sooner than one year after the action of the Legislature.

Article 92

Proposed constitutional amendments shall be accompanied by statements setting forth the reasons therefor and shall be published in the Official Gazette and made known to the people through the information services of the Republic. If more than one proposed amendment is to be voted upon in a referendum, they shall be submitted in such manner that the people may vote for or against them separately.

Article 93

The limitation of the Presidential term of office to two terms, each of six years duration, may be subject to amendment; provided that the amendment shall not become effective during the term of office of the incumbent President.

CHAPTER XIII

TRANSITIONAL PROVISIONS

Article 94

a) Notwithstanding anything to the contrary in this Constitution, any person duly elected to any office provided for under this Constitution and under the laws in force immediately before the coming into force of this Constitution shall be deemed to have been duly elected for the purpose of this Constitution and to have assumed the position so occupied on the date of coming into existence of this Constitution.

b) Notwithstanding anything to the contrary in this Constitution, elections for the President, Vice–President and members of the Legislature, prior to the coming into force of this Constitution, shall be held on the 3rd Tuesday in January 1985. The person so elected President of Liberia shall be inaugurated on the 12th day of April 1985. The President, Vice–President and members of the Legislature who are elected for the first term prior to the coming into force of this Constitution, shall serve their respective terms less approximately three months. This Constitution shall come into force simultaneously with that inauguration.

c) Notwithstanding anything to the contrary in this Constitution, the People's Redemption Council shall by decree convene a session of the newly elected Legislature before the 12th day of April 1985, to enable the Senate and House of Representatives to organize and elect their officers. Such elections shall be conducted in accordance with the rules and procedures laid down by the Legislature under the suspended Constitution until changed by the new Legislature.

d) Any person who, under the laws extant immediately before the coming into force of this Constitution, held an appointment or was acting in an office shall be deemed to have been appointed, as far as it is consistent with the provisions of this Constitution, to hold or to act in the equivalent office under this Constitution until appointments otherwise provided for under this Constitution shall have been made.

Article 95

a) The Constitution of the Republic of Liberia which came into force on the 26th day of July 1847, and which was suspended on the 12th day of April 1980, is hereby abrogated. Notwithstanding this abrogation, however, any enactment or rule of law in existence immediately before the coming into force of this Constitution, whether derived from the abrogated Constitution or from any other source shall, in so far as it is not inconsistent with any provision of this Constitution, continue in force as if enacted, issued or made under the authority of this Constitution.

b) All treaties, executive and other international agreements and obligations concluded by the Government of the People's Redemption Council or prior governments in the name of the Republic prior to the coming into force of this Constitution shall continue to be valid and binding on the Republic unless abrogated or cancelled or unless otherwise inconsistent with this Constitution.

c) All foreign and domestic debts or other loans and obligations contracted by the Government of the People's Redemption Council or Prior governments or any agency or other authority in the name of the Republic of Liberia prior to the coming into existence of this Constitution, shall continue to be binding on the enforceable by the Republic of Liberia.

Article 96

Notwithstanding anything to the contrary in this Constitution:

a) The People's Supreme Court of Liberia and all subordinate courts operating prior to the effective date of this Constitution shall continue to so operate, and the Chief Justice, Associate Justices of the People's Supreme Court and judges of subordinate courts holding appointments in such courts shall continue to hold such appointments after the coming into existence of this Constitution until their successors are appointed and qualified; provided, however, that all judges of subordinate courts shall remain and preside in their respective resident circuits pending the reconstruction of the Supreme Court. The appointment by the President, with the consent of the Senate, of the Chief Justice and Associate Justices of the Supreme Court and judges of subordinate courts, shall be made as soon as possible after the coming into force of this Constitution. The Chief Justice and Associate Justices of the People's Supreme Court and judges of subordinate courts holding office prior thereto, unless reappointed, shall cease to hold office and their function shall automatically devolve upon the newly appointed Chief Justice, Associate Justices of the Supreme Court and judges of subordinate courts, respectively.

b) Where any legal or administrative proceeding has been commenced, or a person seeks action by any authority or one acting under the authority of the Government, that matter may be carried on and completed by the person or authority having power or by his successor-in-office; and it shall not be necessary for any such proceeding to be commenced de novo. Any act completed by any person or authority having power under the existing law shall not be made the subject of review or commenced anew by anyone assuming the authority of that office after the coming into force of this Constitution.

Article 97

a) No executive, legislative, judicial or administrative action taken by the People's Redemption Council or by any persons, whether military or civilian, in the name of that Council pursuant to any of its decrees shall be questioned in any proceedings whatsoever; and, accordingly, it shall not be lawful for any court or other tribunal to make any order or grant any remedy or relief in respect or any such act.

b) No court or other tribunal shall entertain any action whatsoever instituted against the Government of Liberia, whether before or after the coming into force of this Constitution or against any person or persons who assisted in any manner whatsoever in bringing about the change of Government of Liberia on the 12th day of April, 1980, in respect of any act or commission relating to or consequent upon:

(i) The overthrow of the government in power in Liberia before the establishment of the government of the People's Redemption Council;

(ii) The suspension of the Constitution of Liberia of July 26, 1847;

(iii) The establishment, functioning and other organs established by the People's Redemption Council;

(iv) The imposition of any penalties, including the death penalty, or the confiscation of any property by or under the authority of the People's Redemption Council under a decree made by the Council in pursuance of but not limited to the measures undertaken by the Council to punish persons guilty of crimes and malpractices to the detriment of the Liberian nation, the people, the economy, or the public interest; and

(v) The establishment of this Constitution.

SCHEDULE

1. This Schedule shall form and be an integral part of this Constitution and shall have the same force as any other provision thereof.

2. All public officials and employees, whether elected or appointed, holding office of public trust, shall subscribe to a solemn oath or affirmation as follows:

"I.... do solemnly swear (affirm) that I will support, uphold, protect and defend the Constitution and laws of the Republic of Liberia, bear true faith and allegiance to the Republic, and will faithfully, conscientiously and impartially discharge the duties and functions of the office of to the best of my ability. SO HELP ME GOD."

COMPLETED THIS 19TH DAY OF OCTOBER, A. D. 1983 IN THE CITY OF GBARNGA, BONG COUNTY, REPUBLIC OF LIBERIA BY THE CONSTITUTIONAL ADVISORY ASSEMBLY

Edward Binyah Kesselly (Lofa County)
Chairman

Charles H. Williams (Grand Bassa County)
Deputy Chairman

Archibald F. Bernard (Montserrado County)
Secretary General

Richard K. Flumo (Bong County)
Assistant Secretary General

Montserrado County

Stephen H. Kolison, Sr.,
Member
James Nagbe Doe,
Member
James N. Nagbe,
Member
Rocheforte L. Weeks,
Member
Pearl Brown-Bull,
Member
Jonathan E.M. Gibson,
Member
Zoe Ethel Norman,
Member
Walter Yedebabuo
Wisner, Jr., Member

Marshall Territory

R. Francis Okai, Jr.,
Member

Bomi Territory

Samuel Dwelu Hill,
Member
K. Ballah M. Davis, Sr.,
Member

Gibi Territory

David S. Menyongai,
Member
Flomo Shadrach Daniel,
II, Member

Grand Bassa County

A. Wilmot McCritty, I,
Member
Abba G. Karnga,
Member
Thomas L. Griggs,
Member
Joseph L. Barchue, Sr.,
Member

Rivercess Territory

T. Gbegbe Roberto
Dole, Member

Sinoe County

Nelson Wm. Broderick,
Member

Charles N. Wiah,
Member
Lawrence S. Bestman,
Member
Jenkinson T. Nyenpan,
Sr., Member

Sasstown Territory
Dennis J. Weagbe,
Member

Maryland County
Nathaniel Bleh Seton,
Sr., Member
James Klaba Giko,
Member
J. Barney Taylor,
Member
Christian A. Baker,
Member

Kru Coast Territory
Carles Barzee Coffey,
Member

**Grand Cape Mount
County**
A. Kini Freeman,
Member

Christopher K.
Kandakai, I, Member
Ernest K. Metzger,
Member
Victor Lamina Yates,
Member

Grand Gedeh County
Harry T. Faber Nayou,
Member
Philip Koryeyon Deah,
Member
Robert Bloh Toe, Sr.,
Member
Emmanuel B. Neewray,
Member
Doquinee Jarpee
Andrews, Jr., Member

Nimba County
J. Patrick K. Biddle,
Member
John Wiemi Bartuah,
Member
James W. Zotaa, Jr.,
Member
J. Gharmie Sahn,
Member

Jenkins G.W. Wongbe,
Member

Peter A. Gbelia, Sr.,
Member

Stephen B. Daniels, Sr.,
Member

Samuel B. Wogbeh,
Member

Bong County

John Flumo Bakalu, Sr.,
Member

James Y. Gbarbea,
Member

Walter T. Gwenigale,
Member

Salome Giddings-Hall,
Member

Manyu M. Kamara,
Member

Lofa County

Edward S. Mends-Cole,
Member

J. Edward Koenig,
Member

Frederick K. Gobewole,
Member

James M. Hargrave,
Member

Keikura Bayoh Kpoto,
Member

TEST YOUR BRAINS

So, what do you think? You think you've understood some of the key details that you need to talk about the principal, precious documents of the Republic of Liberia? This section of the little book is to tease you about how much you got out of the reading. As was mentioned earlier, if you go through the questions, and don't get all the answers, you can go over the material, again and again.

The main point is that when you go over and over the material, many of the details will stick with you and make you very informed. That is what we want! —When every Liberian gets to know the rights and responsibilities needed to become a valuable Liberian citizen, hopefully, we all will be careful to act in ways to bring peace and protect the peace. When a country is at peace, so many great things can happen!

Let's try that. Shall we?

TEST YOUR BRAINS

1. What is the minimum age a person must be to serve as a Member of the House of Representatives?
    a. 18
    b. 21
    c. 25
    d. 30

2. Every person arrested or detained shall be formally charged and presented before a court of competent jurisdiction within how many hours?
    a. 24 hours
    b. 36 hours
    c. 48 hours
    d. 72 hours

3. The power to prepare a bill of impeachment is solely in the:
    a. House of Representatives
    b. House of Senate
    c. Supreme court
    d. All of the above

4. What provision of the constitutions gives citizens the right to move freely throughout Liberia and to reside in any part of the country?
    a. Article 11a
    b. Article 11b
    c. Article 12a
    d. Article 13a

5. Money shall not be drawn from the Liberia Treasury unless:
    a. An appropriation is made by legislative enactment and upon warrant of the President
    b. The President has issued an Executive Order authorizing such expenditure
    c. The Supreme court has ordered the payment of such money
    d. Any one of the above

6. Who presides over an impeachment trial of the President?
    a. The Speaker of the House
    b. The Senate Pro Tempore
    c. The Vice President
    d. The Chief Justice

7. Who may declare a state of emergency?
    a. Only the President
    b. The President in consultation with the Pro tempore of the Senate
    c. The President in consultation with the Speaker of the House of Representatives
    d. The President in consultation with the Speaker of the House of Representatives and Pro tempore of the Senate

8. Liberia is a unitary sovereign state divided into counties for administrative purposes. The form of government is

a. Democratic
b. Republican
c. Electoral
d. Capitalist

9. Which of the following is a duty of the Vice President?
   a. Speaker of the House of Representatives
   b. President of the Senate
   c. Chairman of the Joint Chief of Staff
   d. Chairman of the President's Cabinet

10. How long must a citizen of the Republic of Liberia be resident in the country or constituency to be represented to be able to become a Representative in the House of Representatives?
    a. Not less than five years
    b. Not less than three years
    c. Not less than one year
    d. Not less than ten years

11. Treason against the Republic of Liberia consists of the following except:
    a. Rebellion against the Republic, insurrection and mutiny
    b. Acts of espionage for an enemy state
    c. Levying war against a neighboring country from Liberia
    d. Conspiring to subvert the Constitution by use of force

12. In an emergency where the Chief Justice and the Associate Justice are not available, the oath or affirmation of the President and Vice president shall be administered by
    a. A judge of a subordinate court of record
    b. The Minister of Justice
    c. The Speaker of the House of Representative
    d. Justice of Peace

13. The writ of habeas corpus shall be suspended
    a. At any time the Executive deems necessary
    b. At any time the Judiciary deems necessary
    c. At any time the Legislature deems necessary
    d. At no time

14. What is the only condition under which Non-citizen missionary, educational and other benevolent institutions shall have the right to own property in Liberia?
    a. As long as a Liberian citizen is a co-owner
    b. As long as that property is used for the purposes for which acquired
    c. As long as such institution continues to provide services to Liberians
    d. As long as such institution continue to pay taxes on the property

15. Which provision of the constitution explicitly gives the Legislature the power to create new counties and other political sub-division, and readjust existing county boundaries
    a. Article 34 (a)
    b. Article 34 (b)
    c. Article 34 (c)
    d. Article 34 (d)

16. Which of the following is NOT true under the Liberian constitution?
    a. All amendments of the constitution or rules of a political party shall be registered with the Elections Commission no later than ten days from the effective dates of such amendments
    b. The Legislature shall enact laws indicating the category of Liberians who shall not form or become members of political parties
    c. All elections of public officers shall be determined by a simple majority of the votes cast
    d. The Elections Commission shall, within thirty days of receipt of the complaint, conduct an impartial investigation and render a decision

17. Of the following powers, which one does NOT belong to the Legislature?
    a. To constitute courts inferior to the Supreme Court
    b. To approve treaties, conventions and such other international agreements
    c. to enact laws providing pension scheme for various categories of government officials
    d. All of the Above Powers belong to the Legislature

18. While attending, going to or returning from a session of the legislature, a Senator or representative cannot be arrested except for the following crime:
    a. Treason
    b. Breach of the peace
    c. Felony
    d. All of the Above

19. What happens if a quorum is not obtained to enable the Supreme Court to hear any case?
    a. A circuit judge in the order of seniority shall sit as an ad hoc justice of the Supreme Court.
    b. The court shall adjourn and wait to reach a quorum before proceeding
    c. The Chief Justice shall nominate someone to replace whoever is absent
    d. None of the Above

20. Which of the following is NOT a method by which a bill becomes law?
    a. Both Houses pass a bill and the President signs it
    b. The House of Representatives passes a bill and the President signs it
    c. Both Houses pass a bill and the President does not sign or return it within 20 days
    d. Both Houses pass a bill, the President vetoes it, and both Houses override the veto

21. The Constitution may be amended under which of the following circumstances?
    a. Whenever a proposal by two-thirds of the membership of both Houses receives the concurrence of two-thirds of the membership of both Houses of the Legislature
    b. Whenever a petition submitted to the Legislature by not fewer than 10,000 citizens receives the concurrence of two-thirds of the membership of both Houses of the Legislature
    c. Any one of the above
    d. None of the Above

22. Which of the following is an Autonomous Public Commission established under the Constitution?
    a. Civil Service Commission
    b. Elections Commission

    c.   General Auditing Commission

    d.   All of the Above

23. The President is required to report to the Legislature on the State of the Republic

    a.   Once a year

    b.   Once a term

    c.   Anytime the President is invited by the Legislature

    d.   In a public address before a joint session of the House and Senate

24. The right of the citizens of Liberia who are 18 years of age or older to vote is protected by which provision of the Constitution?

    a.   Article 77a

    b.   Article 77b

    c.   Article 78

    d.   Article 79

25. There shall be elections of Paramount, Clan and Town Chiefs by registered voters in their respective localities to serve for a term of _____ years

    a.   Two

    b.   Four

    c.   Six

    d.   Eight

Liberia lies on the West Coast of Africa. It covers an area of 37,189 square miles of land and 5,810 square miles of water with a coastline of 350 miles long. The population of Liberia as of the 2008 census is 3.5 million people. The country is divided into 15 political subdivisions or counties. The name Liberia comes from Latin which means free—land of the free. The country was founded in 1822 by the American Colonization Society as the settlement of freed slaves from the United States of America. Prior to the coming of the freed slaves, many indigenous people consisting of sixteen ethnic groups lived on the land. The settlers who became known as the Americo-Liberians and others who joined them after the abolition of slavery formed a government and declared Liberia an independent state in 1847, becoming Africa's first independent republic.

The Americo-Liberians consisting only of five percent of the country ruled Liberia from its founding in 1822 until 1980 when a military coup led by mainly indigenous low-ranking military officers toppled the government headed by William R. Tolbert, a descendant of the freed slaves. Master Sergeant Samuel Kanyon Doe became the new leader and ruled the country for the next ten years. A civil war in which President Doe was killed started during the Christmas season of 1989 and lasted for over a decade. By the time it ended, about 250,000 Liberians were killed, and almost half of the population was either displaced or exiled. The first substantive postwar elections were held in 2005 with Mrs. Ellen Johnson Sirleaf winning as president, and the country has remained peaceful, although vestiges of the war persist even after a decade of peace and democratic rule.